EARLY MOTORBUS
BRITAIN 1904

STEAM ROADCAR
BRITAIN 1857

ELEPHANT
with
HOWDAH
INDIA

RED INDIAN TRAVOIS, N. AMERICA, 17th century

LAND
TRANSPORT

CONTENTS

'Through the Ages'
TRANSPORT

by MURIEL GOAMAN

with illustrations by
FRANK HAMPSON

Publishers WILLS & HEPWORTH Ltd Loughborough
First published 1970   ©   *Printed in England*

TRANSPORT

Today, we can travel and send our parcels by motor-car, train, ship or plane.

Early man had to walk, carrying his own goods. In backward lands men and women still carry burdens on their heads or backs.

Early man made rough sledges out of branches. He could cross a deep river on a floating log. He used branches or his hands as paddles.

Later, men made axes and chisels from stone. These were used to chip out the insides of logs for boats. Sometimes fires were lit in a log to burn out a hollow.

7214 0238 0

Early man learned how to move more quickly on water, as well as on land. The floating log gave him the idea of building his own boats and canoes. He made wooden oars and sails from skins or woven reeds. He found that he could make his boats move as he wished.

This made him more bold. He began to travel across the seas.

The early Britons made boats called 'coracles'. These had a wooden framework so light that they could be carried easily. Coracles are still used in Wales.

We do not know who made the first wheel. We *do* know that wheels were in use nearly 6,000 years ago.

The early people who made them left clay and copper models. These show us what their wheels looked like. They were made of thick pieces of wood joined together.

The axle moved around with the wheels. A cart was tied to the axle with leather thongs.

The wheels were very heavy. After a time someone had the idea of cutting holes in the wheels to make them lighter.

Though clumsy, carts with these disc wheels made transport easier.

The Romans first invaded Britain in 55 B.C.

They found rough tracks, but no proper roads. The British wheeled chariots had to keep to dry, high ground.

The Roman legions needed straight, hard roads, so that they could move fast. They built roads with layers of stones, and paved them.

A column of Roman soldiers held six men abreast. Two columns could pass each other on the new roads.

After the Romans left Britain, the art of road-making was lost for hundreds of years.

Traces of the Roman roads can still be seen in Britain.

Early Roman wagons had disc wheels. These were made stronger by wooden boards.

After a time, wheels were made with rims. The rim was joined to the hub with spokes.

This new wheel was still clumsy, but was much lighter than the disc wheel. Wagons with spoked wheels could carry more weight.

Chariots used in battle had bronze wheels. Horses and mules pulled the Roman wagons and carts.

Two-horse chariots were used for racing.

By the time the Romans came to Britain, boats had become very much larger. Goods could be carried from one place to another by water. Trade was possible with lands across the seas.

Large boats were used to carry soldiers to war. The Romans built galleys to bring their legions to fight Britain. Some of the galleys carried masts and square sails.

The Romans built a 'pharos' or lighthouse at Dover. The light made it safer for the galleys to move at night.

When man learned to tame animals, he not only used them for pulling chariots and carts, he also used them for carrying his goods on their backs. Perhaps the dog was taught to carry the first load. Dog teams are still used in snow-covered countries.

Oxen and horses were tamed to carry packs on their backs, and were called 'pack-animals'. In England, pack-horses were used up to a hundred years ago.

Animals are still used in this way in many lands. Mules, donkeys, camels, elephants and yaks are all 'beasts of burden'. They can carry loads through country-side too difficult for other transport.

During the Middle Ages, the roads in Britain were not much better than muddy tracks. Quite short journeys took many days or weeks.

Poor people had to walk. Rich people travelled on horse-back or in carriages.

Springs for carriages had not been invented then. The wheels jolted over great ruts in the road. The travellers in the carriages became very stiff and sore.

Women from wealthy families were often carried in litters. These were slung between two horses.

In 1565, Queen Elizabeth the First was given a new sort of carriage. The body of the coach was joined to the frame by leather straps. As the coach moved, the body swung to and fro.

This was a great benefit to the traveller; he no longer jolted over every rut in the road. As a result, wheeled traffic became more popular.

No-one knew how to make good roads like those made by the Romans. Roads were still only rough and muddy tracks.

The next improvement came about a hundred years later when the metal spring was invented.

The spring was made of fine steel and shaped like the letter 'C'. It smoothed out the jolting of the carriages, and so these could be made much lighter. These lighter carriages — the stage coach, the post-chaise and the curricle — could move more quickly. They did not damage the road surface.

Sedan-chairs were used in towns. Two men carried each sedan-chair, which was much more comfortable than the Elizabethan litter.

Between 1700 and 1850, the stage coach was the main means of travel between towns. These coaches were pulled by four or more horses. The horses were changed at regular intervals.

Man had always wanted to fly. Early attempts were made with 'wings' of wood and canvas. With these, men jumped off high buildings, but were often injured or killed.

The first men to fly were Frenchmen. They did not use wings but made balloons of paper and linen. These had a hole in the bottom, and were lifted by hot air rising from a fire beneath. In 1783 some Frenchmen flew over Paris in one of these balloons.

Later, a gas called hydrogen was used to fill the balloon. This gas is lighter than air and is still used in balloons today.

Before the building of our modern type of road, much heavy traffic crossed Britain by river. Cities grew up on the river banks. Increase of trade with overseas lands turned these cities into busy ports.

Between the years 1700 and 1800, many canals were cut. They linked up with the rivers. For the first time, boats and barges could move between busy towns in the Midlands and to ports on the coast. A barge was pulled by a horse which walked along a 'tow-path'. Coal and iron could be carried to the factories. Goods could be carried from the factories to the ports for sending overseas.

These 'inland waterways' helped to make Britain wealthy, as trade with other countries grew.

Up to about 1700, wood was used for the building of houses, ships and all wheeled traffic. It was also used as fuel in homes and industries.

By then, most of the forests in Britain had been cut down. When coal became the main fuel, more iron could be produced.

In 1769, James Watt discovered that steam could be used to turn a wheel. In 1804, Richard Trevithick used steam to drive the first successful steam locomotive. It ran on metal rails, and could pull trucks with people and goods. From this grew the railway system we know today.

Soon after the year 1800, a German invented the 'hobby-horse'. This strange machine had a wheel back and front, a seat, but no pedals. The rider had to push himself along with his feet.

This was the beginning of the bicycle as we know it today.

One of the strangest early bicycles was called a 'penny-farthing'. It was so named after coins of the time and because the front wheel was huge and the back wheel tiny. This machine was rather dangerous to ride and very uncomfortable.

The early bicycles had metal-rimmed wheels. The air-filled tyre was invented later.

Railed tracks, often made of wood, were used in Britain in the seventeenth century, mainly in quarries. The tracks were often laid on a slope. Trucks ran down by their own weight, or horses pulled them.

These tracks were called 'tram-roads'. From them came the idea of tramways in towns.

Early trams ran on raised metal rails, but these got in the way of the other traffic. Later, rails were sunk in the ground.

The first passenger trams were pulled by mules and horses. This was in the late nineteenth century. After 1900, most trams had electric motors, and picked up the electric current from overhead wires.

Over the centuries, the design of ships has developed greatly.

After the invention of the steam locomotive in 1804, it was not long before steam was being used to drive ships. By the year 1900, steamships had largely taken the place of ships with sails. They had to carry a large stock of coal for the boilers which made the steam.

The first steamships were driven by paddle wheels. Later, screw propellers were used. The new ships were made of iron instead of wood. Then steel replaced iron for shipbuilding.

The first steam-turbine ship was built in 1897. Many ships today are powered by diesel-oil engines. In America, one has been fitted with nuclear power. The Russians, too, have a nuclear-powered ice-breaking ship.

The first motor-cars were called 'horseless carriages'. These were thought to be dangerous, and an Act was passed in 1864. It said that a man waving a red flag must walk in front of all horseless carriages. This stupid law held up the development of motor-cars in England.

Roads had been greatly improved between the years 1800 and 1900 by the ideas of two men, Telford and Macadam. Early motor cars had wheels like those on horse-drawn carriages, and these stirred up clouds of dust. Tarmacadam had to be laid on the road surface to keep it smooth and hard*.

Later, air-filled tyres were invented. These made the ride more comfortable, and did not damage the road surface.

* *See the Ladybird book — " The Road Makers".*

Man's first flight was in a balloon and experiments with airships were made much later. These were not very successful, though a German airship, the Graf Zeppelin, crossed the Atlantic in 1928.

In 1903, the first petrol-driven aeroplane flight was made in America. The plane was designed by two brothers named Wright. Five years later Bleriot flew across the English Channel in a monoplane.

After the First World War (1914-1918), aeroplanes were used to operate services to most parts of the world.

Until the Second World War however, most travellers still went by train and ship, only using aircraft for very urgent journeys.

George Stephenson built the first public railway in 1825. It ran between Stockton and Darlington*. At first the railway was used to carry coal. Later, stage coaches were fixed onto the railway wagons. Passengers sat in these.

Railways were built to cover most of the country. Steam locomotives later reached speeds over 100 miles an hour. Today, steam locomotives are not being built; diesel and electric locomotives have taken their place. Electric locomotives are faster, smoother and cheaper to run than steam or diesel locomotives. They pick up their electric current from overhead wires.

London's Underground railways (known as 'Tubes') also run on electricity.

* See the Ladybird book — "The Story of Railways".

The invention of the motor car has brought problems on the roads. So many people now use cars for travelling to work or for pleasure.

Most English roads have always been narrow. Many of them have dangerous bends and corners. New motorways and good, modern bridges are now being built. Dangerous bends on old roads are being made straight.

Special mobile police patrol busy main roads to help in case of accidents or traffic hold-ups. All the time, the work of improving our roads goes on.

Aeroplanes have one great drawback. To stay in the air they must travel at high speed. This means they need space to take off and land. Also, they cannot 'stand still' in the air.

To overcome these problems, inventors had the idea of making the wings revolve, so that an aeroplane could 'hover' (stand still) in mid-air, as well as fly normally. It could also then take off and land in a very small space.

This invention was called a 'helicopter' — and many are now used for transport purposes, as well as rescue work over the sea or in difficult, mountainous areas.

During the 1939-1945 war, aeroplanes were made in great numbers, and 'jet' engines came into use.

After the war, faster, bigger and safer aeroplanes were used for travel over long distances. More and more people used them, and cities all over the world built airports specially for these large jet planes.

The large jet passenger planes now include huge 'jumbo' jets carrying three or four hundred people, and airliners flying faster than sound. Sound travels at about 760 m.p.h.

The air space over airports is now becoming almost as busy as our roads. Taking-off and landing must be carefully controlled.

Man has long wanted to be able to travel under the sea.

The problem was to keep all water out of the craft. Deep water exerts great pressure. Some way of withstanding this pressure had to be found.

The first submarines were not very successful. The two World Wars brought big developments in submarines. They are now much safer and are fitted with means of escape if the submarine is unable to surface.

The most up-to-date submarines are powered by nuclear energy. They can stay under the sea for many weeks at a time.

So far, it does not seem that submarines will be very useful for carrying passengers.

Man has learned to travel quickly and easily in the air and over the land and sea. He is now turning his attention to travelling in the space surrounding the earth[*].

We know of the exciting voyages that space-men have made. They have circled the earth. They have brought back photographs showing what Earth looks like from Space.

Now men have landed on the Moon and returned safely. Soon they may be travelling to the planets, Mars and Venus.

* *See the Ladybird book — "Exploring Space".*

12 ENGINED FLYING BOAT
GERMANY 1929

ROMAN MERCHANT
SHIP, 2nd century

FULL-RIGGED
SAILING SHIP
BRITAIN, 19th century

VIKING SHIP
6th century

GALLEON, ENGLAND
16th century